*For Jennifer, Katie,
Thomas and Elizabeth*

**Other Cambridge Reading books
you may enjoy**

Garlunk
Helen Cresswell

Captain Cool and the Ice Queen
Gerald Rose

A Door to Secrets
Tony Mitton

**Other books by J. Burchett
and S. Vogler you may enjoy**

Tower Block Blowdown

Ghost Goalie

Save the Pitch

Once upon a time, a princess knocked on
the door of a royal palace. It was dark and
it was raining. She was bedraggled and
forlorn and in need of shelter.

"Wait a minute," I hear you say, "I know this story. Princess taken in for the night. Sleeps on piles of mattresses. Queen's put a pea underneath as a Proper Princess Test. Princess sleeps badly because she feels the pea. Therefore she's a real princess and can marry the prince. Why should I read it again?"

So I say, "Because that was a load of old rubbish. If you want to hear the true story – read on . . ."

The queen made a great fuss of Princess Elsie. She gave her dry clothes and a plate of sausages.

"What a kind, motherly woman," thought Elsie, stuffing her face with bangers.

She liked the king's dashing moustache and she thought Prince Wilfred was very handsome. It might be worth staying for a while. She didn't hear the queen giving special orders for her bed. She didn't see the gleam in the queen's eye as a platoon of royal servants staggered by with the royal bedding.

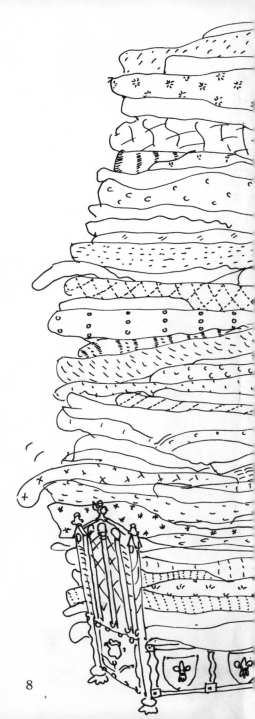

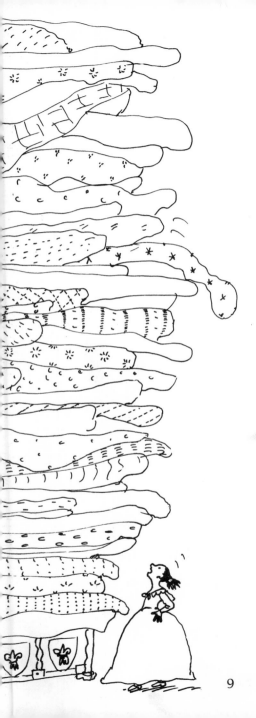

However, when she saw her bed, she nearly said a very rude word. One hundred mattresses soared up to the ceiling. It looked like the north face of the Eiger. Elsie hated heights but it would be rude to complain. So she began the long climb.

"Don't look down," she muttered to herself.

She did have one bad moment. She lost
her footing when she was passing mattress
number fifty-two. She slipped down to
mattress thirty-eight. She hung there for a
minute, wondering if the sausages were
going to come back up.

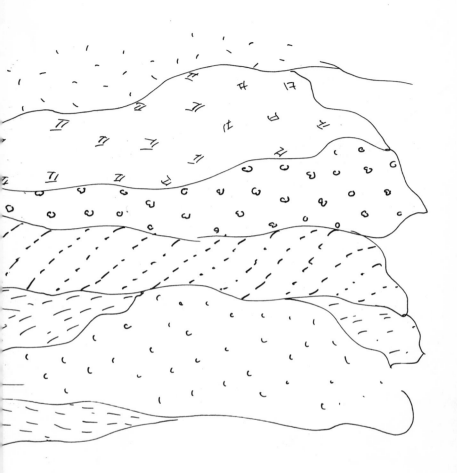

But she wasn't a princess for nothing and at last she got a grip. Finally, she reached the top and collapsed in a heap. But however she lay, she couldn't get to sleep. It felt as if an ostrich egg was poking her in the ribs.

Next morning, a yawning Princess Elsie
was escorted to the royal breakfast room
where the royal family awaited her. She
was in a foul temper. In the cold morning
light, the king's moustache drooped and
he reminded her of a walrus. The queen
was fat and wore too much make-up.
Wilfred was still as handsome as ever but
seemed a bit dim. He started to suck his
thumb. The queen slapped his hand.

"Did you sleep well?" she asked Elsie.

Now, our princess was a well brought up young lady.

"Yes, thank you," she murmured through gritted teeth.

The queen seemed disappointed.

"And the bed?" she asked sweetly. "Was it comfortable? I had a few extra mattresses put on specially."

"Forgive me," said Princess Elsie, stifling a huge yawn, "but I did find it a tiny bit . . . erm –"

"Lumpy?" prompted the queen.

"Yes. It was like trying to sleep on a tortoise . . ."

Princess Elsie wished she'd kept her mouth shut. How rude of her! They'd probably throw her out before she'd finished her cornflakes. But to her astonishment the queen leapt into the air, knocking Wilfred's egg and soldiers off the table.

"I knew we'd find her one day!" she shouted. "A real princess!"

It's a fairy tale come true!

"What's going on?" asked Princess Elsie.

"My dear, dear Elspeth," said the queen, shaking Elsie's hand vigorously. "Congratulations! My husband and I have been searching for years to find a real princess, a proper and fitting bride for our son. We placed the Royal Pea under your mattress because it has always been said that a true princess would still be able to feel the Royal Pea. Just think – one hundred mattresses and still you felt the pea."

"Yeah, yeah, yeah," I hear you say. "So the princess marries the prince and lives happily ever after. What's so different about that?"

"Don't count your chickens before they're hatched. Or should I say, don't count your royals before they're hitched. Stop interrupting and read on."

Elsie stared.
She felt her
mouth fall open.
She shut it quickly.
"You mean . . ." she
spluttered. "You mean, that
even though I'd fallen in a ditch,
been chased by a flock of killer sheep
and walked seventeen miles in high heels,
you still carried out your silly test? Why
didn't you look me up? I'm in the book
– Elspeth, Proper Princess. I'm just after
Elephant, Nellie the. And just before
Ethelred the Unsteady (Royal Acrobat.
By Appointment.)."

The royal family were completely taken aback. Princess Elsie ought to have been delighted to get such a catch. The queen recovered quickly, however.

"You are overwrought, my dear. You need some rest. Eat your cornflakes. Then have a doze on the sofa. Just one cushion and no vegetables," she added, laughing at her own joke.

The queen spent the day congratulating herself on her cleverness. She'd found a real princess for Wilfie. Mothers of neighbouring princes would be green with envy. She couldn't wait until the next Royal Mothers' Union meeting, so she phoned around.

The king announced it to his mates over a darts match in the pub.

Prince Wilfred wrote to his pen-pal in Latvia and told her all about it.

Dinner that evening was a
sumptuous feast. A celebration.
The queen plunged straight in.

"Now – the wedding dress," she said.
"Silk would be perfect, with a satin train.
Covered in pearls."

Elsie looked her straight in the eye.

"I am not prepared to discuss any
wedding plans," she said.

The king dropped his spoon in the gravy
and Wilfred choked on a sprout. No-one
ever contradicted Mummy. Elsie was
furious. This family must be quite mad.
Suddenly she realised that in her temper

she had been squeezing a walnut in her clenched fist. It gave her an idea.

Next morning, the queen was in full flow with her wedding plans.

"I've booked the archbishop for ten fifteen on Thursday. The reception will be at the palace." She glared at the king. "Not in the darts room at the 'Dog and Duck'. And the bridesmaids –"

I was looking forward to that.

Princess Elsie interrupted.

"How did you sleep, Wilfred?" she asked sweetly.

It's going to be all right, thought the queen. We'll have no more trouble from her.

Prince Wilfred looked up from his latest letter to his pen-pal in Latvia and gazed devotedly at Elsie – as he'd been told to.

When he didn't reply, the queen pinched him – hard.

"Ow! Oh . . . ah . . . like a log, my precious," he simpered, rubbing his arm.

"And the bed, my sweetness, was it comfortable?"

"Rather, poppet. Never had a better night's kip."

"I see," said Princess Elsie, coldly.
"Right then, I'll be on my way. Thank you
for having me. If you're ever near my
castle . . . don't bother to look me up!"

The royal family sat with their mouths
open. It was as if she had suddenly turned
into a frog.

"What!" spluttered the queen at last.

"Let me explain," said Elsie. "No –
much better, let me show you."

She got up from the table and marched out of the room. The others followed. She led the way to Prince Wilfred's bedchamber and lifted the mattress to reveal a walnut, two almonds, three conkers – and a pineapple, just to be absolutely sure.

"Seeing as no-one asked me about the wedding," said Princess Elsie,

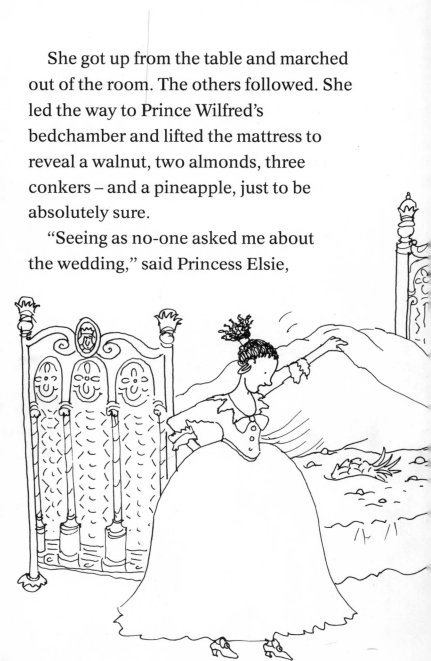

"I decided to sort it out for myself."

She looked round at them. The king had turned green. Wilfred was sucking his thumb and twisting his hair vacantly. The queen was opening and closing her mouth like a large, blubbery goldfish.

"If you will only take on a real princess for your son," explained Elsie, "it is equally fair that I can only take Wilfred on if he's a real prince. And he obviously isn't. He didn't feel the Royal Walnut, the Royal Almonds, the Royal Conkers or the Royal Pineapple. He didn't pass the Proper Prince Test!"

She swept out of the room and out of their lives. Perhaps she married and perhaps she didn't, but she definitely, most assuredly, lived happily ever after.

"So there never was a wedding," I hear you say.

"Oh yes there was. Prince Wilfred did get married. This is how the story you know came to be told."

No sooner had the royal door slammed
behind Princess Elsie than Wilfred
popped his thumb out of his mouth.

"Well, I'd better be packing then," he said.

"Packing?" snapped the queen.
"You are the most stupid –"

"Shut up, Mummy, and listen for
a change. If I'm not a proper prince
I can marry the girl of my choice.
I'm off to Latvia to propose to Min."

"To whom?" thundered the queen.

"Miniouska Mousanova, my
pen-pal. Must dash. Toodle pip."

Five minutes later Prince
Wilfred was spotted heading
through the royal
shrubbery with
an arctic tent,
a map and
a toothbrush.

Five days
later, the

archbishop was
dragged out of bed, on
his day off, to perform the
royal wedding ceremony.

And, as the bride just happened to be allergic to peas, the queen managed to convince everyone that Princess Min was a Proper Princess.